I0840077

Are You... Ready For It?

First things first. We're back for season two of our favorite love birds. America's Royal Couple. Tayvis. Miss Americana and the Football Prince.

The first season was magical··· watching the games to catch a glimpse of our favorite blondie and to see what outfit she was wearing every week, how she would represent Travis and the Chiefs more and more with each of those outfits (Ah! The outfits!), and her accessories, who would be in the suite with her, when would the families meet... but wouldn't it be nice to know what they're actually doing out on the field and understanding what our favorite #87 does best? Don't you also want to impress your football loving significant other, family, and friends with your football knowledge?

Here are a few basics to get you started:

1) Teams: NFL football is played between two teams, each consisting of 11 players. The offense is trying to score. The defense is trying to keep the offense from scoring.

2) Coin Toss: Before kickoff, a coin toss determines which team starts with possession of the football- one team will start on offense, the other will start on defense. The winner gets to decide if they want to be offense or defense.

3) Objective: The goal is to advance the ball into the opponent's end zone (the painted areas at each end of the field) to score points.

4) Downs: Teams have four downs (chances) to advance the ball 10 yards.

5) Offensive Strategies: Teams use various plays, like running or passing, to move down the field strategically.

"The players gonna play, play, play, play play"
-Taylor Swift, "Shake It Off (Taylor's Version)"

6) Scoring: Points are earned by crossing the opponent's goal line for a touchdown (6 points), extra point (1 or 2 possible points) after a touchdown, or kicking a field goal (3 points).

7) First Down: Gaining 10 yards or more in four downs earns the team a new set of downs. What is a down? It's an "attempt" or a "try".

8) Turnovers: Intercepting passes or recovering fumbles gives the opposing team possession of the football. You take the ball away from the other team and your team is now on offense.

9) Special Teams: This unit handles kickoffs, punts, and field goals during the game.

10) Clock Management: Teams must manage the game clock to maximize their offensive and defensive opportunities. You have 40 seconds to start a play from when the last one ends or you get a penalty.

11) Defensive Tactics: The defending team aims to stop the offense through tackles, blocks, and strategic plays.

12) Timeouts: Teams can call timeouts to stop the game clock and discuss strategies. Each team gets 3 per half.

13) Punting: If a team can't advance the ball, they may choose to punt (a form of kicking) to the other team.

Let's dive a little deeper...

Offense:

There are two main parts of a football team- offense and defense.
We are mostly concerned with the offense because our new favorite football player (Travis!) plays on offense. The primary job of the offense in football is to move the ball down the field and score points. The offense consists of various players, each with specific roles and responsibilities, working together to achieve these objectives. Here are the key aspects of the offense's job in football:

Go Chiefs!

Scoring Points:

The ultimate goal of the offense is to score points by crossing the opponent's goal line or kicking the ball through the goalposts- that big yellow "H" shaped thing at the end of the field.
Touchdowns, (Call the amateurs and cut em from the team...Oh sorry, I got carried away!) worth six points, are scored by running or catching the ball into the opponent's end zone.Field goals, worth three points, can be scored by successfully kicking the ball through the opponent's goalposts.

Advancing the Ball:

The offense aims to move the ball down the field by running or passing plays. They have four downs (attempts) to advance the ball at least 10 yards. If successful, they earn a new set of downs. Various offensive positions, such as quarterbacks, running backs, and wide receivers, play specific roles in advancing the ball. And don't forget about the Tight End!

Executing Plays:

The offense uses a playbook (sometimes you will see the head coaches holding a version of these on the sidelines, and they kind of look like an iHOP menu) containing a variety of plays designed to deceive and outmaneuver the opposing defense. Plays can involve running the ball, where a player carries it forward, or passing the ball, where the quarterback (or sometimes another player in the case of Travis that one time. He did used to be a quarterback, after all!) throws it to a receiver.Effective communication and execution of plays are essential for success and WINNING!

Protecting the Quarterback:

The quarterback is a crucial player on the offense responsible for passing the ball and making key decisions. The offensive line's primary job is to protect the quarterback from the opposing defense, giving them time to make accurate throws.

Clock Management for Offense:

The offense manages the game clock to control the pace of the game and prevent the opposing team from having too much time to score.
Timeouts and strategic plays are used to optimize the remaining time in each half.

Adjusting to Defensive Strategies:

The offense must read and adapt to the opposing defense's formations, coverages, and blitzes. Quarterbacks often make audibles or changes to the play at the line of scrimmage based on the defensive alignment. This is all of the yelling that the quarterback does before the ball is snapped. The more yelling, and the crazier the words, the greater chance that he is calling an audible.

Red Zone Efficiency:

When the offense enters the opponent's red zone (inside the 20-yard line), it aims to maximize scoring opportunities, often requiring precision and creativity. In essence, the offense's job is to outsmart, outmaneuver, and outscore the opposing defense by effectively moving the ball down the field and converting opportunities into points. Teamwork, strategy, and execution are key components of a successful offensive unit.

Defense:

We definitely don't care as much about the defense since they are the sworn enemy of Travis (and Travis' brother, Jason, incidentally), but you should at least understand what they are trying to do during the game. The primary job of the defense in football is to prevent the opposing team's offense from scoring points and to gain possession of the ball.

The defensive unit is responsible for stopping the offensive team's progress, creating turnovers, and ultimately protecting their own end zone. Here are the key aspects of the defense's job:

Preventing Scoring:

The primary objective of the defense is to prevent the opposing offense from scoring points. This includes stopping them from reaching the end zone for a touchdown and blocking field goal attempts.

Tackling and Stopping the Run:

Defenders aim to tackle ball carriers, typically running backs, and prevent them from gaining significant yardage. Stopping the run is crucial to limiting the offense's options and forcing them into less favorable situations.

Defending Against Passes:

Defensive players, especially defensive backs and linebackers, work to disrupt and intercept passes. This involves covering receivers closely, deflecting passes, and intercepting the ball to regain possession.

Sacking the Quarterback:

The defense aims to sack the quarterback by tackling them behind the line of scrimmage before they can throw the ball. Sacks disrupt the offensive rhythm and can result in lost yardage for the offense.

Creating Turnovers:

The defense seeks to create turnovers by forcing fumbles, intercepting passes, or recovering loose balls. Turnovers provide the defense with an opportunity to switch the momentum and give their own offense a chance to score.

Defending Against the Red Zone:

Inside the red zone (the area between the defense's 20-yard line and the goal line), defenses intensify their efforts to prevent the offense from scoring touchdowns. Red zone defense is crucial for limiting the opponent's point production.

Reading Offensive Plays:

Defensive players and coaches analyze the opposing offense's formations, tendencies, and play-calling to anticipate and counter their strategies. This involves reading the quarterback's intentions and adjusting defensive alignments accordingly.

Pass Rush and Blitzing:

Defensive linemen and linebackers engage in pass rushing to put pressure on the quarterback, disrupting their ability to make accurate throws. Blitzing involves sending additional defenders to overwhelm the offensive line and create chaos in the backfield.

Coverage Schemes:

Defensive backs employ various coverage schemes, such as man-to-man or zone coverage, to limit the effectiveness of receivers and prevent big plays down the field.

Clock Management for Defense:

Defenses may strategically use timeouts to manage the game clock, especially in critical situations late in each half.

Adjusting to Offensive Formations:

The defense must adapt to the offensive formations and personnel on the field, making adjustments to counter the opponent's strengths.

Goal-Line Stands:

In crucial situations, the defense may face a goal-line stand, where they try to prevent the offense from scoring when close to the end zone. In summary, the defense's job is to disrupt, deny, and control the opposing offense, ultimately preventing them from scoring points and creating opportunities for their own team to succeed. Tactical awareness, physical prowess, and effective communication are essential for a successful defensive unit.

Key Positions:

There are many positions in football- definitely more than you care to learn about, but there are some that you need to know about to sound like you know what you're talking about.

We'll focus on the position that we care about the most... GO TAYLOR'S BOYFRIEND! Travis is a tight end, and he's arguably one of the best tight ends in the league, and maybe of all time (he's kind of a big deal!). A tight end (TE) is a versatile player who lines up on the offensive line. The tight end's role combines elements of both offensive lineman and wide receiver, making them crucial assets in various offensive strategies. Here are the primary responsibilities and roles of a tight end:

Receiving Threat:

Pass-catching Ability: Tight ends are often used as receiving targets in the passing game. They have good hands and the ability to catch passes thrown by the quarterback. This versatility makes them a valuable asset in short to intermediate passing routes.

Red Zone Target:

Due to their size and often favorable matchups against defenders, tight ends are frequently targeted in the red zone (the area between the opponent's 20-yard line and the goal line) for potential touchdown receptions.

"I wanna be your end game. I wanna be your first string."
- Taylor Swift, "End Game"

Blocking:

Run Blocking: Tight ends are expected to be effective blockers, especially in the running game. They may line up next to offensive tackles and help create running lanes for the ball carrier by blocking opposing defensive linemen and linebackers.

Pass Protection:

In certain situations, tight ends may be asked to assist offensive linemen in protecting the quarterback during passing plays. This can involve blocking defensive ends or blitzing linebackers.

Versatility:

Motion and Flexibility: Tight ends can line up in various positions, including at the end of the offensive line (attached to the tackle), in the slot (between the offensive line and wide receivers), or split out wide like a wide receiver. This flexibility allows offenses to create mismatches against the opposing defense.

H-Back Role:

In some offensive schemes, the tight end might function as an H-back, a hybrid position that combines the blocking responsibilities of a fullback with the receiving abilities of a tight end. This further expands their role in both the running and passing game.

Yards After Catch (YAC):

Running with the Ball: Tight ends are often used in plays where they catch short passes and have the opportunity to gain additional yards after the catch. Their combination of size, strength, and agility can make them difficult to bring down, turning short completions into significant gains.

Recognition of Defensive Schemes:

Reading Defenses: Tight ends need to understand defensive formations and coverages to adjust their routes and blocking assignments accordingly. This football IQ is crucial for success in both the passing and running game. In summary, the tight end is a versatile player who contributes to both the passing and running aspects of the game. Their ability to catch passes, block effectively, and create mismatches on the field makes them valuable assets in NFL offenses. Travis is talented, versatile, strong, athletic and smart!

Other important positions:
Quarterback (QB):

Often considered the most important position, the quarterback is the team's primary playmaker and leader. The quarterback is responsible for passing, handoffs, and making crucial decisions on the field. A skilled quarterback can significantly impact the team's offensive success. Patrick Mahomes (#15) is Travis' quarterback, and he's considered to be one of the best (if not the best) in the NFL. He (and his wife, Brittany) were at Taylor's show in Amsterdam when she sang arguably one of the most Tayvis coded surprise song mash ups EVER, and we're pretty sure we saw Travis shed some tears.

Offensive Tackle (OT):

Offensive tackles protect the quarterback's blind side and create running lanes for the ball carrier. Left tackles, in particular, are critical for shielding a right-handed quarterback's vulnerable side.

Defensive End (DE):

Defensive ends are crucial in both pass rushing and run defense. They apply pressure on the quarterback and play a key role in stopping running backs. Effective DE's can disrupt the opposing offense and create turnovers.

Cornerback (CB):

Cornerbacks cover wide receivers, aiming to prevent successful passes and create interceptions. Skilled cornerbacks can neutralize top receivers and limit the opposing passing game.

Middle Linebacker (MLB):

The middle linebacker is often the quarterback of the defense, responsible for reading offensive plays, making adjustments, and leading the defensive unit. They play a crucial role in both run and pass defense.

Wide Receiver (WR):

Wide receivers are primary targets for the quarterback in the passing game. Skilled receivers can stretch the field, make difficult catches, and turn short passes into big gains. Rashee Rice (#4) is a Chiefs' WR that you'll want to watch.

Running Back (RB):

Running backs carry the ball and contribute to the ground game. A reliable running back can control the clock, gain crucial yards, and provide balance to the offense. Isaiah Pacheco (#10) is the Chiefs starting RB, and he's one of the best in the NFL.

Safety (FS/SS):

Safeties are the last line of defense, responsible for preventing big plays and providing coverage deep in the secondary. Free safeties (FS) and strong safeties (SS) work together to secure the defensive backfield. Justin Reid (#20) is the Chiefs starting Safety.

Kicker (K) / Punter (P):

Special teams play a crucial role in field position and scoring. Kickers are responsible for field goals, extra points, and kickoffs, while punters focus on pinning the opposing team deep in their own territory. Harrison Butker, who you probably heard about during the offseason for his not so savory comments about women, is the kicker for the Chiefs.
That's all I have to say about that except that he's probably not a Swiftie, so...

Center (C):

The center is a vital part of the offensive line,
snapping the ball to the quarterback and anchoring
the line during both running and passing plays.
Fun fact: This was the job of Travis' brother, Jason,
who just retired and will be working for ESPN on
Monday Night Football, hopefully talking about our
all time favorite couple when Travis' team
plays on Monday Night! Fun fact #2: Jason is more than
likely to become an NFL Hall of Famer for playing center,
since he was one of the best to ever play that position.

Defensive Tackle (DT):

Defensive tackles play a key role in stopping the run and
disrupting the opposing offense. They provide interior
pressure on the quarterback and help control the
line of scrimmage. Chris Jones (#95), who you have
probably seen if you've been paying attention, is
the Chiefs' best Defensive Tackle.

While these positions are often highlighted for their
importance, football is a team sport, and success relies
on the collective effort of all players on the field. The
effectiveness of a team is often determined by
the synergy and coordination among players
across various positions.

Scoring:

This is the best part of the game and what makes Taylor cheer- well, when the Chiefs score, that is. There are a few ways to score during a game.

Touchdown (6 points):

The primary way to score is through a touchdown. A touchdown occurs when a player with possession of the ball crosses the opponent's goal line into the end zone. This can be achieved through running or catching a pass. A touchdown is worth six points. Either the offense or the defense can score a touchdown. The defense can score a touchdown if they either intercept the ball or recover a fumble and get the ball into the endzone in the same play. When Travis scores a touchdown, he can sometimes be seen doing his famous Archer pose, which Taylor likes to do during the TTPD set when she sings, "But Daddy I Love Him," but, so far, only when Travis is in attendance.

"I've been the archer, I've been the prey..."
- Taylor Swift, "The Archer"

Extra Point (1 or 2 points):

After scoring a touchdown, the scoring team has the option to attempt an extra point. From the 15-yard line, they can kick the ball through the opponent's goalposts for 1 point, or they can attempt a 2-point conversion from the 2-yard line by running or passing the ball into the end zone again. The 2-point conversion isn't as easy as it sounds, which is why it isn't done as often.

Field Goal (3 points):

A field goal is scored by kicking the ball through the opponent's goalposts. This can be attempted from anywhere on the field, but it is most commonly attempted on fourth down when a team is within range of the goalposts. A successful field goal is worth 3 points.

Safety (2 points):

A safety is an uncommon but impactful scoring play. It occurs when the defense tackles an offensive player with possession of the ball in their own end zone. The team that scores a safety is awarded 2 points, and they also gain possession of the ball through a free kick from their own 20-yard line.

Turnovers:

Besides when Travis gets shoved by another player, something else that makes Taylor sad/mad is when Travis' team commits a turnover. A turnover refers to a change of possession where the defensive team gains control of the ball from the offensive team. Turnovers are significant moments in a game, often having a crucial impact on the outcome. Several ways exist for turnovers to occur:

Interception:

An interception happens when a defensive player catches a pass intended for an offensive player. This defensive player gains possession of the ball for their team, and the offense loses its chance to score on that play. (AKA: the quarterback throws the ball to someone on the other team!)

Fumble:

A fumble (aka Don't Drop the Baby!) occurs when a player has possession of the ball and loses it, either by dropping it or having it knocked away by an opponent. Any player on either team can recover the fumble, and the team that recovers gains possession.

"Maybe we got lost in translation, maybe I asked for too much"
-Taylor Swift, "All Too Well (Taylor's Version)"

Muffed Punt or Kickoff:

If a player on the receiving team fails to catch a punt or kickoff cleanly and the ball hits the ground, it becomes a live ball. If a member of the kicking team recovers, they gain possession, resulting in a turnover.

Turnover on Downs:

If the offense fails to advance the ball the required distance (10 yards) in four downs, the ball is turned over to the opposing team at the spot where the last play ended.

Blocked Field Goal or Punt:

If a defensive player blocks a field goal or punt attempt, the ball is live, and either team can recover it. If the defense recovers, it's a turnover.

Interception Return for a Touchdown:

Otherwise known as a Pick Six. When a defensive player intercepts a pass and returns it into the opposing end zone for a touchdown, it not only results in a change of possession but also scores points for the defense.

Safety:

While not a turnover in the traditional sense, a safety results in the defense being awarded two points, and then the team that was scored upon must kick the the ball from their 20-yard line.
A safety occurs when the offense is tackled in its own end zone, giving the ball to the opposing team. Not only do they get 2 points but they get the ball back and immediately get the chance to score again!

Turnovers are critical moments that can swing momentum in a game. The team with a strong defense capable of creating turnovers often gains a significant advantage. On the other hand, the offensive team strives to protect the ball and avoid turnovers, as they can lead to scoring opportunities for the opposing team. The ability to capitalize on turnovers and limit mistakes is a crucial aspect of success in a game.

Penalties:

Did you see the game last season when Travis' quarterback (Patrick) got really mad and threw his helmet and started cussing on the sideline? He was very upset (understatement!) at the referees for a penalty that they called on one of his teammates. I know A LOT has happened since then, and maybe you forgot all about that, but it was a BIG DEAL. Penalties can cause problems for football teams and they should be avoided if possible. Penalties are infractions of the rules that result in the imposition of yards, downs, or the awarding of a first down to the opposing team, which means they get 4 more chances to try to score.

Penalties can impact the flow of the game and create strategic advantages or disadvantages for the teams involved. Here are some common penalties in football:

Offensive Holding:

Penalty: 10 yards from the spot of the foul (where the penalty took place). Occurs when an offensive player grabs or restricts an opponent to prevent them from making a play. Commonly called on offensive linemen during running plays or pass protection.

False Start:

Penalty: 5 yards from the line of scrimmage. Occurs when an offensive player moves before the ball is snapped, disrupting the normal progression of the play. Commonly called on offensive linemen and occasionally on other players.

Defensive Pass Interference:

This is a big one! Penalty: Automatic first down for the offense and the ball is placed at the spot of the foul (again, where the penalty happened). Occurs when a defensive player interferes with an eligible receiver's ability to catch a pass. This can include grabbing, pushing, or impeding the receiver's progress.

Illegal Block in the Back:

Penalty: 10 yards from the spot of the foul. Occurs when a player blocks an opponent in the back, away from the direction of the play. This penalty is often called on special teams or during interception or fumble returns.

Roughing the Passer:

This one makes the players really mad because they are usually super protective of their quarterback. Penalty: 15 yards from the line of scrimmage and an automatic first down. Occurs when a defensive player makes illegal contact with the quarterback after they have thrown a pass. This includes hits to the head, late hits (a hit or tackle that happens after the play has ended), or landing on the quarterback with excessive force.

Unsportsmanlike Conduct:

Penalty: 15 yards from the end of the play or the spot of the foul. Called for behavior deemed contrary to the principles of good sportsmanship, such as excessive celebrations (dancing for too long in the end zone- Travis likes to do this, and we LOVE to see it! Unless he gets a penalty), taunting, or fighting. Sometimes, a player is removed from the game for this penalty (usually for helmet to helmet contact or fighting).

Delay of Game:

Penalty: 5 yards from the line of scrimmage. Occurs when the offense fails to snap the ball before the play clock expires.

Offensive Pass Interference:

Penalty: 10 yards from the line of scrimmage. Occurs when an offensive player interferes with a defensive player's ability to defend against a pass. This includes pushing off, blocking downfield before the pass is caught, or creating separation through illegal means. This doesn't get called very often but when it does, Travis gets super mad.

Illegal Formation:

Penalty: 5 yards from the line of scrimmage. Called when the offense lines up with an incorrect number of players on the line of scrimmage.

"Are we out of the woods yet, are we out of the woods yet, are we out of the woods?"
-Taylor Swift, "Out of the Woods, (Taylor's Version)"

Offside:

Penalty: 5 yards from the line of scrimmage. Occurs when a defensive player crosses the line of scrimmage before the ball is snapped.

These are just a few examples of the numerous penalties in football. The specific rules and penalties can vary, but understanding these common infractions can enhance your appreciation for and understanding of the game. Not to mention, some of the reasons why they throw those little yellow flags on the field ALL. THE. TIME.

So, what's the big deal anyway?

Why does Travis do what he does? Besides the fact that he (obviously) loves it! He, like all of the other players in the league, wants to win a championship (The Super Bowl).

The objective of an NFL season is to determine a champion among the 32 teams in the league. The season is structured to provide a competitive framework where teams play a series of games to earn a spot in the playoffs.

"They'd say I hustled, put in the work"
-Taylor Swift, "The Man"

The key objectives of an NFL season include:

Regular Season:

The regular season consists of 17 games for each team. During this phase, teams compete against opponents from their own conference and inter-conference matchups. The objective is to accumulate the best win-loss record to qualify for the playoffs. The season is 18 weeks though because teams get a "bye week," or a week off. Remember when Travis went to Argentina and was in the tent with Taylor's dad and got to hear her sing "Karma is the guy on the Chiefs comin' straight home to me" live and in person for the very first time ever and we all went berserk?! That was during his bye week, and maybe that was your Roman Empire...

Divisional Titles:

Winning the division is a significant goal for teams during the regular season. Each conference is divided into four divisions, and the team with the best record in each division earns a divisional title. Division winners are guaranteed a spot in the playoffs.

Wild Card Spots:

Teams that don't win their division but have strong records may still qualify for the playoffs as wild card teams. Wild card spots go to the teams with the best records that didn't win their respective divisions.

Playoffs:

The playoffs consist of a single-elimination tournament. A total of 14 teams (seven from each conference) qualify for the playoffs. The top seed in each conference receives a first-round bye (or week off), while the other six teams face off in the Wild Card Round.

Conference Championships:

The winners of the Divisional Round advance to the Conference Championships, where the top two teams from each conference compete for the conference title. The winners earn a spot in the Super Bowl. The Chiefs won their conference championship last year against the Baltimore Ravens. It was after this game that we saw Taylor join him on the field to celebrate with (and kiss!!!) him for the first time.

Super Bowl:

The Super Bowl is the culmination of the NFL season and is the championship game where the champions of the AFC (American Football Conference) and NFC (National Football Conference) face off. This is the ultimate goal of every single team in the NFL.
ALL. SEASON. LONG.

This is what they play for. The winner of the Super Bowl is crowned the NFL champion for that season, and it's a very big deal. Some players never even get to play in the Super Bowl, let alone win one.
Travis has won THREE!

"Cheers chanted, cause
they said there was no chance trying to be
the greatest in the league. Where's the Trophy?
He just comes running over to me"
-Taylor Swift, "The Alchemy"

I mean... that's pretty much exactly what happened last season, right??

Individual Achievements:

In addition to team goals, individual achievements are also significant in the NFL. Players strive to achieve personal milestones, such as leading the league in various statistical categories, earning Pro Bowl selections, and being recognized with awards like the MVP (Most Valuable Player).

Entertainment and Fan Engagement:

The NFL season aims to provide entertainment for fans across the world. The league's popularity is built on the excitement and drama of the games, the passion of the fanbase, and the spectacle of events like the Super Bowl.

Player Development and Evaluation:

NFL teams use the season to develop their players, evaluate talent, and make strategic decisions for the future. Rookies and young players often get opportunities to showcase their skills and contribute to the team.

Economic Impact:

The NFL season has a substantial economic impact, contributing to the league's revenue through various channels such as ticket sales, broadcasting rights, merchandise, and sponsorships.

In summary, the primary objective of an NFL season is to determine the league champion through a competitive and structured process that includes a regular season, playoffs, and ultimately the Super Bowl. The season also serves as a platform for individual and team achievements, fan engagement, and economic success for the league.

Speaking of Merchandise...

Did you know that after Taylor was seen for the first time at Travis' game in September of last year, that the sales for Travis' jersey went up by 400%.
FOUR. HUNDRED. PERCENT.
The sales spiked on the same day that Taylor was spotted in the suite with Mama Kelce for that game. This is just one example of the "Swift Effect".

The "Swift Effect":

The "Swift effect" refers to the noticeable impact Taylor has had on the NFL, particularly during the 2023 season when her appearances at games and her public relationship with Travis garnered significant media attention. Here are some specific aspects of the Swift effect on the NFL:

Increased Viewership: Taylor's presence at games, especially Kansas City Chiefs games, drew a large number of viewers who might not typically watch football. Her fans (US!!) tuned in to catch glimpses of her, leading to a spike in viewership ratings for those games.

Merchandise Sales:

On top of the increase in sales for Travis' jersey, there has been a huge surge in Chiefs/Swiftie crossover merchandise. Everything from tshirts, sweatshirts, hats, stickers... etc. I was at Disney World last year and saw people wearing NFL "Taylor's Version" t-shirts among other NFL/Swiftie merch.

Social Media Buzz:

Taylor's appearances and her relationship with Travis generated substantial social media buzz. This included trending topics, memes, and discussions that extended beyond typical sports audiences, reaching a broader demographic.

Cultural Crossover:

The Swift effect highlighted a cultural crossover between music and sports. It brought together fans of both domains (even the dads, Brads & Chads), creating a unique blend of entertainment and sports culture. I have seen photos and videos of people wearing Kelce (both Travis and Jason!) jerseys at the Eras Tour. There are stories of dads and daughters watching football together. There are Swifties who were already Chiefs fans whose worlds have collided and are now living their best lives watching their favorite player and their favorite performer. Swifties are huge fans of Travis & Jason's New Heights podcast, which is mostly about football. It's also hilarious and a glimpse into the relationship of these two brothers. Plus... if you're lucky, you can sometimes hear Travis talk about "Tay".

Extra Credit

Now that you know A LOT more about football than you did before, it's time to learn a little bit more about Travis' team. You probably know, at the very least, that Travis plays for the Kansas City Chiefs and that he wears number 87 (the year Jason was born).

The Kansas City Chiefs are a part of the American Football Conference (AFC) West division in the NFL. The AFC West consists of four teams.

Kansas City Chiefs (KC):

The Chiefs were founded in 1960 and have been a successful franchise, winning multiple division titles and Super Bowls, including Super Bowl IV, Super Bowl LIV, Super Bowl LVII, and now, most famously for Swifties- Super Bowl LVIII.
Their coach, and now our coach, is Andy Reid- nicknamed "Big Red". Andy is known as somewhat of a mastermind of football. Sounds like someone else we know.
Fun fact: Taylor knew Andy before
she knew Travis.

"Where's the Trophy? He just comes running over to me"
-Taylor Swift, "The Alchemy"

The Chiefs have won the AFC West title for the past eight years. They have played in 6 Super Bowls and have won 4. Travis has played in 3 Super Bowls and has won 3. He has 3 Super Bowl rings. He and the Chiefs won the Super Bowl in 2023 against his brother's team, The Philadelphia Eagles, and in 2024, the Chiefs won the Super Bowl against the San Francisco 49ers with Taylor in attendance. Remember how we were all doing Swiftie math to figure out what time she would finish her concert in Tokyo, how long it would take to fly to Vegas, and if she would make it to the game? In case you missed it: She made it!

What They Wear & Where They Play:

They wear red, yellow, and white. When they are playing at home, they wear red jerseys and white pants. On the road, they wear white jerseys and red pants the majority of the time. Their helmets are red with a white arrowhead with the "KC" logo inside. They play at Arrowhead stadium. Remember when Travis told the world that he told Taylor that he saw her rock the stage in Arrowhead and that he wanted her to come see him rock the stage in Arrowhead?

That was her first time to see him play in person,
and that was when they were introduced as a couple
to the world. Some would say that was their
"hard launch" as a couple. Others call the moment
he stepped on to the Eras Tour stage in a full tux to
perform along side Taylor and her dancers their
official "hard launch". Either way, I think we
would all agree that they are more than launched
at this point! We all saw the video
of him when he first spotted her in the
suite with his mom (Mama Kelce), and that trademark
crinkling eye smile of his when he mouthed
the words, "Dang, she's right there." That's what
we *think* he said. There's no audio, so we're relying
on lip reading here. It's almost like he was as
shocked as all of the rest of us were to see
her at his game.

Bonus points: Travis has the most receiving yards
of any Kansas City Chief in history-
GO TAYLOR'S BOYFRIEND!

"You'll be the prince, and I'll be the princess. It's a love
story, baby, just say, 'yes'"
-Taylor Swift, "Love Story (Taylor's Version)"

Other Teams in the AFC West (AKA Arch Rivals!):

Denver Broncos (DEN):

The Denver Broncos were established in 1960 as a charter member of the AFL (American Football League) before the AFL-NFL merger. The Broncos have won multiple AFC West titles and have achieved success on the national stage, winning multiple Super Bowls.

Las Vegas Raiders (LV):

Formerly known as the Oakland Raiders, the team moved to Los Angeles in 1982 and then back to Oakland before relocating to Las Vegas in 2020. The Raiders have a rich history and have won multiple division titles and Super Bowls.

Los Angeles Chargers (LAC):

Originally based in Los Angeles, the Chargers later moved to San Diego before relocating to Los Angeles again in 2017. The Chargers have had success in the AFC West and have produced notable players throughout their history.

These four teams compete within the AFC West division, playing each other twice during the regular season. The team with the best record in the division earns the AFC West title and secures a spot in the playoffs. The AFC West has been known for its competitive matchups and rivalries, making it a closely watched division in the NFL.

When will we see Taylor this season?

Taylor finished the European leg of The Eras Tour on August 20th, and now she has nearly 2 months off. This gives her LOTS of opportunities to attend Travis' games before she starts touring again in October in the US, starting off in FLORIDA!!! If last season is any indication of the lengths she will go to see her man play, I'm betting she will be at every possible game that she can be, and we can be sure that she will have some of her celebrity besties in tow. Will we see Jason and Kylie (Jason's wife, who we also LOVE!) in the suite now that he is retired? How many new and different Chiefs or Kelce themed outfits and accessories will she show off this season?

"And this is when the feeling sinks in. I don't want to miss you like this. Come back, be here" -Taylor Swift
"Come Back, Be Here (Taylor's Version)"

September 2024

Sunday	Monday	Tuesday	Wednesday	Thursday	Friday	Saturday
1	2	3	4	5 **Ravens vs Chiefs**	6	7
8	9	10	11	12	13	14
15 **Bengals vs Chiefs**	16	17	18	19	20	21
22 **Chiefs vs Falcons**	23	24	25	26	27	28
29 **Chiefs vs Chargers**	30					

October 2024

Sunday	Monday	Tuesday	Wednesday	Thursday	Friday	Saturday
		1	2	3	4	5 **Travis' Birthday**
6	7 **Saints vs Chiefs**	8	9	10	11	12
13	14	15	16	17	18 **Taylor in Miami**	19 **Taylor in Miami**
20 **Taylor in Miami** **Chiefs vs 49ers**	21	22	23	24	25 **Taylor in NOLA**	26 **Taylor in NOLA**
27 **Taylor in NOLA** **Chiefs v Raiders**	28	29	30	31		

"So make the friendship bracelets,
take the moment and taste it."
-Taylor Swift, "You're On Your Own Kid"

November
2024

Sunday	Monday	Tuesday	Wednesday	Thursday	Friday	Saturday
					1 **Taylor in Indy**	2 **Taylor in Indy**
3 **Taylor in Indy**	4 **Bucs vs Chiefs**	5	6	7	8	9
10 **Broncos vs Chiefs**	11	12	13	14 **Taylor in Toronto**	15 **Taylor in Toronto**	16 **Taylor in Toronto**
17 **Chiefs vs Bills**	18	19	20	21 **Taylor in Toronto**	22 **Taylor in Toronto**	23 **Taylor in Toronto**
24 **Chiefs vs Panthers**	25	26	27	28 Thanksgiving	29 **Raiders vs Chiefs**	30

December
2024

Sunday	Monday	Tuesday	Wednesday	Thursday	Friday	Saturday
1	2	3	4	5	6 **Taylor in Vancouver**	7 **Taylor in Vancouver**
8 **Taylor in Vancouver** **Chargers v Chiefs**	9	10	11	12	13 **Taylor's Birthday**	14
15 **Chiefs vs Browns**	16	17	18	19	20	21 **Texans vs Chiefs**
22	23	24	25 **Chiefs vs Steelers**	26	27	28
29	30	31				

"I go back to December all the time"
-Taylor Swift, "Back to December (Taylor's Version)"